THE MISSING MAN

FINDING A MISSING MAN

ANUDIP GHOSH

Copyright © Anudip Ghosh
All Rights Reserved.

This is dedicated to each and everyone of us who are living in the earth. I want to my earthmen to be a good citizen of their respected country with moral values and spiritual knowledge.

Contents

Foreword

Forewords are not available.

Preface

This is a book which has a lot of meaning with moral values and spiritual knowledge. The poems have different meanings related to the topic.

Acknowledgements

Deepest thanks to my many patient, generous and hopeful readers. I hope my dear readers would interestingly like my book first book of publision. I thank God for giving me different ideas that came in my brain. I would once again thank everyone for reading my book.

Prologue

Prologues are not available.

1. THE MISSING MAN

A man of the kind,
Of the stunning find.
Was lost from his house,
Was topping over the browse.
We quested him,
Was named Tim.
He was mad,
Was a little fat.
He stayed in Australia,
Over the continent Oceania.
He was a doctor,
Lived in Rockter.
We searched him over,
Was a topper.
We searched him in bedroom,
Lacking in Living room.
Near the Baker's street,
As a horrible feet.
We stopped finding him,
And started to throw food on him.
A big bread butter,
Over the matter.
Was very tensed,
Over the fringed,
We again started to find him,

Took two hours for him.

But haven't founded,

That innocent Tim.

He had two sons,

Haven't any guns.

We informed the police,

By the colleagues.

Anew tomorrow, we winced perceiving him,

At the house of his brother Kim.

Then, at his uncle's,

And of his sister's and aunt's.

But was still lacking,

He was the heir apparent of the king,

The king sends his army,

After his madness of creamy.

He liked to eat chicken kofta,

Wore Indian kurta.

The smell of the chicken kofta always attracted him,

But, this time it did not attracted him.

Perceiving, perceiving,

Crying, Crying,

But was not perceived,

We saw a man just looking for him.

We thought he was Tim,

We called him.

When turning his face,

We understood that he was not Tim.

We called his friend,

Was not as trend.

We asked him,
But the same reply was given by him.
Three days later,
We found him fatally dead.
But, suddenly he woke me up from sleep,
I later understood that it was a dream.

2. THE CAT AND THE RAT

The cat was roaming,
While the rat was sleeping.
In Mr. Gooling's house,
Were the pets from Brouse.

The cat stayed in the cat house,
While the rat stayed in the hole.
The fat bad cat stayed in the room of less use,
While the clever rat has a mole.

The cat was black,
While the rat was brown.
The cat had a lack,
Of good qualities.

One day, the cat thought,
Would eat the rat.
The fish given to the cat that Googling bought,
Was rotten for one year.

The cat planned,
While the rat himself canned.
The cat knew about the plan,
From the hearing of Clan.

Clan was a dog,
While the rat jog.
Clan was a friend of him,
Who stayed near a light beam.

As the cat dared to come,
The rat was worried for some.
The cat understood where he is,
So, the cat threw the can.

But before that could happen,
He put a lemon inside it.
When the cat opened the can,
He said to himself "I'm a fool".

The cat ran around the house,
The cat found him.
Both of them ran like a browse,
But the rat was tired.

The cat has a fear of Clan,
Clan beats him relentlessly.
So, the rat went to Clan,
The cat then ran fearfully.

The rat told Clan,
About the story.
The dog made a trap,

When the cat came, he was fallen into the trap.

Clan beat him fiercely,
And told him "Apologise or fight".
Then the cat apologised him,
The rat forgave him.

The dog them told to be friends,
And forget everything.
Both agreed,
And both lived happily to the end of their lives.

3. THE INSTANCE OF THE NIGHT

Mr. Michael was returning to home,
Was talking over a phone.
In the strange night,
Of the horrible sight.

The road had a curse,
That he was not awarese.
The curse was that,
A monster would kill that person flat.

No one was there,
Was feeling scare.
That night was eerie,
But the atmosphere was airy.

The call was about one hour,
And it ended there.
Then he suddenly felt scar,
Of the eerie situation there.
Then suddenly he saw a gigantic shadow,
Was about a four feet tall.
Was a long fellow,
Like a forty feet mall.
The monster was red in colour,
Who likes to eat bread.

Who wore a turban which is red,
Looked like a muscle man.

He wore a shirt which is black,
But had a lack,
Of good qualities,
Then came different natural calamities.

He wore a pant,
Which is blue.
But, he can't,
Know how to moo.

Then Mr. Michael tried to hide,
For about two hours.
The monster saw him,
And ran like a horse.

Michael was a policeman,
Who tried to shoot him.
But, unable to hurt him,
He decided to go to Dr. Serious.

Dr. Serious was scientist,
Who had tight fist.
He is the best scientist in the world,
But was a little mad.

The police told him,

About the story.
The mad fellow told him,
To take any skin or hair of the gigantic monster.

The police immediately gave him,
A hair of monster.
But in no time,
The monster came.

Destroying his lab,
That the scientist's fab.
Ran like a browser,
There came a garden of flower.

After running for half an hour,
They were tired.
They jumped into the river far,
And the monster fired.

But the scientist and the fellow,
Escaped from the river.
They went to the secret lab,
Of the scientist's fab.

The scientist tested the hair,
In the monster's fear.
He immediately created the antidote,
To kill the monster.

They put it in the syringe,
In AK 47 arrange.
Instead of the bullets,
They put the syringes.

They appeared before him,
Wearing flying helmet then.
First, to know where he is weak,
They threw stones and pebbles on him.

They saw that,
That the fat.
Monster was weak,
In his chest.

They threw fire on him,
Which drew his attention.
Towards the fire,
He put some water.

With the monster's attention to the fire,
They threw syringes antidote.
But was running,
Trying to hire.

They had 100 syringes,
But unfortunately, 99 of them were missed.
Only one syringe,

That could kill the monster fished.

They pulled up his chin,
Tipped and shooting it fin.
Which targeted his spine,
Shoot it which fatals the fine.

This brought an end,
To the monster.
Which made them popular,
By killing the monsters.

Once again with creating an antidote,
Made him famous.
Along with Mr. Michael,
Made them famous.

The government provided them,
With a house and a lab.
To the police and the scientist,
Which made them happy.

With this, they were made heroes,
Like sparrows.
With the likes,
Which made them feel proud for their rest of their lives.

4. THE REVOLTED ACTION

Our country was safe,
From the rounded cape.
For a very long time,
About half a centenary rhyme.

Our biggest enemy was Robert,
Who was the President in the nearby country of Fevernert.
But he was defeated and killed in a battle,
About a dispute of cattle.

He was a close friend of the very far Kingdom of Lilyver,
The mighty enemy of our country too; King Johniver.
He wanted to take revenge,
Against my country fringe.

King Johniver made a plan,
With his fellow ministers.
King Johniver marched with his army,
With the head of the army; Mr. Abey Blan.

He attacked my country,
With his huge army.
He attacked and killed our King Jack V,
And the powers of our country Veron were transferred to King Johniver.

He appointed George Dreamland as Governor General,
And appointed Tom Fire as Army General.
George was a cruel man,
Whereas, Tom had a tan.

All the regional kings, peasants, zamindars and people were unhappy,
For ruling our country happy.
We wanted to remove the Lilyver Crown from our country,
That had a small pantry.

I was in the army,
According to the law was necessary.
I also served in the army of King Jack V,
Which gave me a plan.

I had good relationship with five of the kings,
They suggested me to be the leader of revolt that would start its wings.
I immediately resigned from the army,
I sent many letters to all the regional kings about the revolt.

About a month, no revolts were going on,
Then, they all proclaimed me as the central leader.
All the soldiers of the regional kingdoms were fighting on,
In various parts of the country.

The Lilyvers captured 386 sepoys,
In various parts we fought battles.
We defeated and released our 386 sepoys,

And we yelled "We marched into the fire!"

We string in in our arms,
We marched into the fire.
We threatened their arms,
We marched into the fire.

We were almost going to win,
But due to the defeat in Furigle.
Our plan was shattered,
I escaped to a nearby jungle.

I trained my own army,
With their help of the tribals.
Now, I'm strong enough,
To fight the fables.

We slowly disarmed the armies,
With the help of many families.
We marched into the fire.
We marched into the fire.

Infront of the eyes of Johniver,
With the tears of sepoys in Lilyver.
We captured Jocker, Keinver and other big cities,
While eating patties.

We marched into the fire.
We marched into the fire.

Surrounding the capital city of Horizon,
And I fought the Battle of Horizon.

The fight did not last for long,
As they were killed in action.
Only King Johniver was left,
Who escaped into the jungle and left.

I with my senses,
Saw the footprints of Johniver.
I followed there,
And saw him.

I and he again started the battle,
I with my archery skills threw arrows onto him ridding on my cattle.
I was saved by a narrow escape,
By my helmet.

I pierced an arrows on his armour,
He went down of his cattle.
I went on to throw about 20 arrows.
Which surrounded him.

And finally with the twenty-first arrows fatals him,
Which laid him.
Onto the ground,
For once and forever to rest.

Then, heard by news of the demise of King Johniver,

Everyone was happier,

Than before,

And finally, the population made me the King of Veron.

For my slogan of "We marched into the fire!

We marched into the fire!"

And for my capacity,

Of fighting this very long revolt.

5. I WISH

I wished that every people on the earth should get food,
I wished that every people should have good deeds.
I wished that every people should be religious,
I wished that every people should have faith in God.

I wished that every people should live their lives happily,
I wished there should be peace in the world.
I wished that war should not occur,
I wished that whites does not discriminate the blacks.

I wished that we could see the souls,
I wished that we could see God.
I wished that all livings beings should live long,
I wished that every people should have houses like mansion.

I wished that Covid virus would be disappeared,
I wished that no people should have diseases.
I wished that India would be the greatest country in the world,
I wished that everyone should fulfil their dreams.

6. LANGUAGE OF HUMANITY

When a country is been created,
That country is been depreciated.
Without humanity,
For a very long infinity.

The countries are losing,
The sight of kindness, honest.
But are growing,
The qualities of evil, dishonest.

We can make the better world,
With the language of humanity.
But of some people,
It is becoming a place of evility.

People are fighting unnecessarily,
Without saying sorry.
The lights are being deemed,
Day by day's framed.

The solution is,
To make people's,
Showing the path of goodness,
Rather than evilness.

Please make the world,
A better place to live in,
Otherwise, our earth is burning,
Which fatal the countries.

The End

If you want to contact me. You are free to contact me.

Phone : +91-9073088543

E-mail : anudipajoy@gmail.com